Concrete Mixers

by Charles Lennie

ABDO
CONSTRUCTION
MACHINES
Kids

Visit us at www.abdopublishing.com

Published by Abdo Kids, a division of ABDO, P.O. Box 398166, Minneapolis, Minnesota 55439.

Copyright © 2015 by Abdo Consulting Group, Inc. International copyrights reserved in all countries. No part of this book may be reproduced in any form without written permission from the publisher.

Printed in the United States of America, North Mankato, Minnesota.

032014

092014

 PRINTED ON RECYCLED PAPER

Photo Credits: iStock, Shutterstock, Thinkstock

Production Contributors: Teddy Borth, Jennie Forsberg, Grace Hansen

Design Contributors: Dorothy Toth, Renée LaViolette, Laura Rask

Library of Congress Control Number: 2013952433

Cataloging-in-Publication Data

Lennie, Charles.

 Concrete mixers / Charles Lennie.

   p. cm. -- (Construction machines)

ISBN 978-1-62970-016-8 (lib. bdg.)

Includes bibliographical references and index.

1. Concrete mixers--Juvenile literature. 2. Construction equipment--Juvenile literature.   I. Title.

629.225--dc23

2013952433

Table of Contents

Concrete 4

Concrete Mixers 10

Concrete Mixer Parts 12

Pouring Concrete 18

More Facts 22

Glossary 23

Index 24

Abdo Kids Code 24

Concrete

Concrete is a building **material**.
It is very important for
construction jobs.

Concrete is a **mixture** of cement and water. Stones and rocks are mixed in too.

Concrete begins as a wet
material. When it dries,
it is hard.

Concrete Mixers

Concrete mixers bring

concrete where it is needed.

11

Concrete Mixer Parts

The driver sits in the **cab**.

The **frame** holds the **drum**.

The drum holds the concrete.

drum

cab

frame

13

The **drum** turns to move the concrete. This keeps the concrete from hardening.

The driver delivers the concrete to the site.

Pouring Concrete

Concrete mixers tip and **pour** the concrete.

Other concrete mixers use a
pump to move the concrete.

More Facts

- A long time ago, horses pulled concrete mixers.

- Some form of concrete has been used for hundreds of years. Egyptians used a concrete **mixture** to build the pyramids.

- Pumper trucks help concrete mixers to deliver the concrete high above the ground at high-rise construction sites.

Glossary

cab – where the driver sits to drive and control the machine.

drum – a large barrel that holds the wet concrete.

frame – the structure made of parts joined together. The frame supports the entire body.

material – anything used for construction, or making something else.

mixture – a combination of two or more different things.

pour – to let flow.

Index

cement 6

concrete 4, 6, 8, 10, 14, 16, 18, 20

construction 4

driver 16

drum 12, 14

engine 12

frame 12

pump 20

uses 10, 14

abdokids.com

Use this code to log on to abdokids.com and access crafts, games, videos and more!

Abdo Kids Code:
CCK0168